A Guide to Shameless Happiness

WILL ROSS

ISBN-13: 978-1499769241
ISBN-10: 1499769245

DEDICATION

To Cindy with love and thanks.

CONTENTS

AUTHOR'S NOTE

This book is designed to provide accurate information in
regard to the subject matter covered. It is distributed with the
understanding that it is not a substitute for psychological,
medical, or other professional services. If expert assistance or
counseling is needed, the services of a competent professional
should be sought.

1. THE TOP FIVE MISSED OPPORTUNITIES FOR HAPPINESS

Are you missing out on happiness? Most of us want to be happy. But every day millions of people miss the opportunity to be happy. These are opportunities that are easy to find. Yet time after time, day after day many people fail to take advantage of them. Are you one of them?

What are these opportunities? Let's take a look.

Time alone. The time you spend by yourself is a great opportunity to be happy. Think of all the fun and creative things you can do when no one else is around. Yet many people are miserable when they're on their own.

Time with friends and family. Friends and family can enrich our lives and provide love and companionship that we can't get on our own. But for many people their relationships with their friends and family are more like a war zone.

Time with a special friend or lover. Most of us have a number of friends and acquaintances. And we also have one or two people with whom we are particularly close. The time we spend with these close friends and lovers can be among the happiest times of our lives. Yet many people miss out on this opportunity for happiness by constantly arguing with their

1

lover. Or worse, many people don't have a "special someone" in their lives.

Time at work or school. Most of us spend a large chunk of our waking hours at work or school. Your career and education give you the best opportunity to engage in rewarding activities. But too many people find their work to be a drudge or highly stressful. They get very little satisfaction from their work.

Recreation time. When you're away from work or school you have ample opportunity to go out and have fun, to do the things you really enjoy doing. Yet many people squander their recreation time by doing too little with it or doing things that are ultimately harmful.

You have the opportunity to be happy every day. But if you're like most people, you probably don't make the most of these opportunities. It's time to make a change. It's time to grab these opportunities and squeeze every ounce of happiness that you can from them.

Yes, you have many opportunities to be happy. But let's be realistic. It's not always easy being happy. We seem to have an unending list of unpleasant jobs to do; we have bills to pay and not enough money to pay them; we get sick or lose our jobs; and we have people in our lives that are difficult to get along with.

On top of that, we live in a world of tragedy: earthquakes, famine, poverty, pollution, crime, violence, war, corruption, greed, unemployment, bigotry, disease, racial and religious intolerance, hurricanes, and homelessness, etc.

In the face of all these difficulties, it's not surprising that so many people are miserable much of the time.

The philosophy of shameless happiness is that you don't have to be miserable. Shameless happiness is a commitment you make to yourself to refuse to be miserable, while unapologetically and unreservedly making yourself happy at every opportunity. Shameless happiness is the pursuit of an ethical, rewarding, and joyous life that is guided by compassion and reason.

2. DO YOU RECOGNIZE THE TWO EARLY WARNING SIGNS OF LONG-TERM UNHAPPINESS?

There is no doubt about it. Life provides many opportunities for happiness. But there is also much to be sad about. While sadness is understandable and appropriate, many people go beyond sadness. Many people show the early warning signs of long-term unhappiness. What are these warning signs?

The two signs that show someone is headed towards a lifetime of misery are (1) unhealthy negative emotions and (2) self-defeating behavior.

Unlike other animals, humans experience a wide range of emotions. Some emotions, such as happiness and excitement, are positive. Others, such as sorrow and grief, are negative. As well as being either positive or negative, our feelings can be appropriate and healthy or inappropriate and unhealthy.

Healthy negative emotions are an appropriate response to negative events. They let you know that something is wrong and they encourage you to make positive changes in your life. But unhealthy negative emotions have no beneficial side-effects.

Here's how you can tell if you are experiencing an

unhealthy negative emotion:

- Do you feel much worse than the situation really calls for? For example, do you feel depressed instead of sad, afraid instead of careful, enraged instead of annoyed, hurt instead of disappointed, ashamed instead of regretful?

- Do your feelings push you to do things that are unhealthy or that get you into trouble? For example, do you smoke, drink too much alcohol, or over eat? Do you procrastinate on important tasks or get into unnecessary arguments with authority figures?

- Do your feelings stop you from doing the things you want to do? For example, do you avoid talking to people you would like to meet; do you put off long-range projects, such as writing a book, because you're afraid of the work involved or the possibility that the end product won't be good enough?

In short, unhealthy negative emotions are extremely painful and counter-productive. Very often unhealthy negative emotions are accompanied by self-defeating actions.

Self-defeating behaviors are actions that harm you or that get in the way of your long-term happiness. Self-defeating behaviors include unhealthy addictions, unhealthy lifestyle choices such as a poor diet along with exercise avoidance, unassertiveness, a self-limiting social life, wasting money on things you don't need, and procrastination, etc.

If you recognize any of these early warning signs in yourself, then the chances are that you are setting yourself up for long-term unhappiness.

The good news is that it doesn't have to be this way. Even in this world, with all its troubles, you don't have to be miserable. You can turn your life around, reach your goals, and be happy – shamelessly happy.

3. WHAT EVERYBODY OUGHT TO KNOW ABOUT HAPPINESS

Many people believe that they have no control over their emotions – that their feelings are a direct reaction to whatever is going on in their lives. But if you think about it, you can easily see how wrong they are. Consider the following scenarios.

- Two 37-year-old twin brothers are flying from Los Angeles to New York. All other things being equal, who is likely to be nervous: the one who believes that flying is boring, or the one who believes that flying is dangerous?

- Two mothers discover that their 17-year-old daughters have been having sex with their boyfriends. All other things being equal, who is likely to be the more upset: the mother who believes that young people absolutely must wait until they are married before having sex, or the one who believes it isn't the end of the world if they have sex before they marry?

- Two young men are in a bar talking to women, trying to pick them up. All other things being equal, who is more likely to be upset if he is rejected: the one who believes it's disappointing – but hardly tragic – to be rejected, or the one who believes he couldn't stand to be rejected?

By thinking through these scenarios, it's not difficult to see that our beliefs influence our feelings. In short, you feel the way you think. If you have happy thoughts you will feel happy; if you have angry thoughts you will feel angry; and if you have fearful thoughts you will feel afraid.

Feeling the way you think has one very important ramification: If you change your thoughts you can change your feelings.

The lesson is clear. By monitoring and adjusting your thinking, you can stubbornly refuse to be miserable about anything. And you can choose to be happy.

4. HERE'S A METHOD THAT IS HELPING MILLIONS TO FIND HAPPINESS

Millions of people around the world have discovered that they can change their feelings by changing their thoughts. Their discovery is due largely to the pioneering work of the American psychologist Dr Albert Ellis who, in 1955, developed a radical new form of psychotherapy which is now known as rational emotive behavior therapy (REBT). Dr Ellis was able to reach a wide audience through his prolific writing including best sellers such as *A Guide to Rational Living* and *How to Stubbornly Refuse to Make Yourself Miserable about Anything – Yes Anything!*

To demonstrate the link between our beliefs and our feelings and behaviors, Albert Ellis created the ABC model. Here's how it works.

A. Something happens.

B. You have a belief about the situation.

C. You have an emotional reaction to the belief.

Here's an example that shows the ABC model in action.

Something happens, (for example, someone cheats you out of money) and you react (for example, you get angry).

Remember that getting cheated does not cause the anger.

It's your beliefs about the fraud that make you angry. In simple, ABC terms we have the following:

A. Something happens (in this case, fraud).

B. Attitude or belief (about the fraud).

C. Reaction as a result of the belief (anger).

Here's another example that shows how changing your beliefs changes your feelings:

A. Your employer falsely accuses you of taking money from her purse and threatens to fire you.

B. You believe, "She has no right to accuse me. She's a bitch!"

C. You feel angry.

If you had held a different belief, your emotional response would have been different:

A. Your employer falsely accuses you of taking money from her purse and threatens to fire you.

B. You believe, "I must not lose my job. That would be unbearable."

C. You feel anxious.

The ABC model shows that A (what happens) does not cause C (your feelings). It is B (your beliefs) that causes C. It is not your employer's false accusation and threat that make you angry; it is your belief that she is a bitch and has no right to accuse you. It is not her accusation and threat that make you anxious; it is your belief that you must not lose your job, and that losing your job would be unbearable.

5. DO YOU MAKE THESE TWO TRAGIC ERRORS OF JUDGMENT?

It's not what happens to you that makes you upset, it's your opinion of what happens to you, your point of view. Whenever something happens, you decide whether or not it is a good thing or a bad thing – you assess the situation and form an opinion about it.

Frequently, whenever we make a judgment about a situation we don't like, we go overboard in our opinion. In fact, there are two very common mistakes that people make when forming their point of view of an unfortunate situation:

- They exaggerate how bad the situation is, and
- They make a demand that the situation must not exist.

The most common exaggerations occur when people tell themselves that they cannot stand the situation. They convince themselves that the situation is awful, practically the end of the world.

The expression "I can't stand it" is an exaggeration. Literally, it means "this situation will kill me." We may not like certain conditions and situations, but very few of them are fatal.

When you tell yourself that you can't stand a situation, you reduce your ability to cope with it. You become overwhelmed by your setbacks because you convince yourself that they will lead to your death.

Another happiness-destroying exaggeration is the claim that some situations are awful or terrible. These words are meaningless; they don't refer to any known quality. Some situations are bad, others very bad. You can, if you like, invent a scale of badness, on which you rate situations from 1% to 100% bad. All unpleasant and inconvenient situations will fall somewhere on this scale.

But when you rate something as awful or terrible, you put it outside the scale. You make it 101% bad, or worse. It's like saying that someone is more than dead, or over-pregnant. It doesn't make sense. Nothing is terrible or awful.

The second mistake people make when forming a judgment is to demand that the situation not exist or that it be different from the way it is or the way it might be in the future.

Demands usually involve using the words "must," "should," "have to," or "got to," etc.

When you demand something (e.g., success, popularity, fairness, convenience, etc.) you are acting like a dictator and a tyrant. It's as though you expect the world – and everyone in it, including yourself – to obey your wishes.

The problem with demands is that they ignore reality. When you use words like "should," "must" and "ought" it is as though you are creating a Law of the Universe that must always be observed. Unfortunately, the universe does not work that way.

When you don't get what you believe you must have, you doom yourself not only to certain disappointment but – worse – to unhealthy negative emotions and self-defeating behavior.

6. HERE'S A QUICK WAY TO MURDER YOUR MISERY

If you feel the way you think, and if demands and exaggerations in your thinking make you upset, then what is the best way to get rid of your demands and exaggerations?

The answer is that you argue with yourself. You ask yourself questions about your demands and exaggerations. The questions you ask will demonstrate that your demands and exaggerations are false. Once you have seen that they are false, you replace them with more reasonable judgments and opinions about your situation.

Is there one question that will get to the heart of the matter? There certainly is! Here's the question to ask: **Where is the proof?**

Where is the proof that I can't stand the situation?

Where is the proof that it's awful – more than 100% bad?

Where is the proof that it's the end of the world?

When you start looking for proof, you'll see that there is none; you'll see that your opinion of the situation is exaggerated nonsense.

You ask yourself the same question about your demands:

Where is the proof that this should not be happening?

Where is the proof that I have to do what I want to do?

Where is the proof that I must have what I want?

Again, when you start looking for proof, you'll see that none exists; you'll see that your demands are nothing but a futile attempt to set yourself up as king or queen of the universe. Although you may strongly want the situation to be different, it does not have to be the way you want it. Sadly, the world does not operate according to your dictates.

Let me show you an example so you can see how to question your demands and exaggerations.

Roger is a 20-year-old college student. Recently, after promising the class there would be no more writing assignments, Roger's English professor told the class that they would have to write one more essay before the end of the term. Roger was furious. He argued with the professor and put off writing the essay.

A. Having to write an extra essay.

B. Not yet known.

C. Angry, argumentative, and procrastinating.

Do you remember the two early warning signs of long-term unhappiness: Unhealthy negative emotions and self-defeating behavior? Roger is quite clearly demonstrating both of these signs.

We know that it wasn't the professor or the essay that made Roger angry – it was his opinion of the professor and the writing assignment that was upsetting him. Roger was telling himself, "It's not fair. I can't stand being lied to. He has no right. He should stick to his word. It's terrible that an English professor – of all people – would lie to his students. I'd like to beat the living daylights out of him. I shouldn't have to write another essay."

Did you notice all the demands and exaggerations? Let's put Roger's opinions where they belong in the ABC model.

A. Having to write an extra essay.

B. I can't stand being lied to.

He should stick to his word.

It's terrible for an English professor to tell a lie.

I shouldn't have to write another essay.

C. Angry, argumentative, and procrastinating.

Anybody would be upset if they made as many demands and exaggerations as Roger has here. Fortunately, Roger knows how to change his beliefs by asking for proof. The first step is to add D to the ABC model. D means to dispute, to question, to argue. Remember, the first step in handling exaggerations and demands is to ask, "Where is the proof?"

D. Where is the proof that I can't stand being lied to?

D. Where is the proof that he must stick to his word?

D. Where is the proof that it's terrible for a professor to tell a lie?

D. Where is the proof that I shouldn't have to write another essay?

Having asked these questions, the next step is to answer them. We write our answers at point E of the ABC model.

D. Where is the proof that I can't stand being lied to?
E. There is no proof. The fact that I'm sitting here writing this proves that I can stand being lied to. Being lied to is inconvenient but it's hardly fatal.

D. Where is the proof that he must stick to his word?
E. There is no proof. He doesn't have to stick to his word. If there were a law of the universe requiring him to stick to his word he would have done so. Since he didn't stick to his word, it is obvious that no such law exists.

D. Where is the proof that it's terrible for a professor to tell a lie?
E. There is no proof. It's certainly unfortunate that my professor lied to me, and having to write another essay is a significant inconvenience, but it's not the end of the world and it's definitely not terrible.

D. Where is the proof that I shouldn't have to write another essay?
E. There is no proof. Much as I'd like to, I do not make the rules. If my professor wants another essay from me, so be it! Instead of whining and complaining about it, I had better get on with writing the essay and getting it over and

done with.

Summary of the ABCDE Method of Finding Shameless Happiness
<ul><li>Something unpleasant happens.</li><li>You form an exaggerated and demanding opinion of the situation.</li><li>Your beliefs cause an unhealthy negative emotion and/or self-defeating behavior.</li><li>You ask "Where is the proof?"</li><li>You answer the questions.</li></ul>

7. NOW YOU CAN FIND HAPPINESS WITHOUT SPENDING A DIME

It is when you write your answers at point E that you become less upset, get rid of your unhealthy negative emotions, and start acting in ways that help you to reach your goals and be happy. Point E, your answer to the question posed at D, is the starting point for a whole new outlook on life.

Using the ABCDE method takes only a few minutes of your time; you can use it practically anywhere, any time; and best of all, it's free, it won't cost you a dime. Surely it's worth taking a few minutes out of your day to form a new outlook that allows and encourages you to pursue a rewarding, ethical, and joyous life.

Your new outlook on life will free you of the two early warning signs of long-term unhappiness; it will give you the freedom and the motivation to make your dreams come true. Since this new outlook is so important, it's worth taking a few minutes to make sure you get it right.

There are certain things in life that most of us want or don't want. For example some of the things you want or don't want may include the following:

- I want to be successful.

- I want to be popular.
- I want my friends to be nice to me.
- I don't want to do household chores.

It's perfectly natural to have desires like these. We get into trouble when our wishes are threatened and we exaggerate how bad the threat is and demand that it not exist.

B. I must be successful.

B. It's awful to be unpopular.

B. I can't stand it if my friends are not nice to me.

B. I shouldn't have to do household chores.

These kinds of beliefs lead to unhealthy negative emotions and self-defeating behaviors. As we have already seen, the best way to get rid of these demands and exaggerations is to question them.

D. Where is the proof that I must be successful?

D. Where is the proof that it's awful to be unpopular?

D. Where is the proof that I can't stand it if my friends are not nice to me?

D. Where is the proof that I shouldn't have to do household chores?

How well you answer these questions will determine how effectively you're able to eliminate your unhealthy negative emotions and start acting in ways that help you to achieve your goal of happiness.

The best answers have two parts to them. The first part acknowledges what you want or don't want. The second part rejects the demands and exaggerations. The two parts are joined together by the word "but".

E. I want to be successful but there is no reason why I must be successful.

E. I want to be popular but it isn't awful to be unpopular.

E. I want my friends to be nice to me but I can stand it if they're not nice to me.

E. I don't want to do household chores but there's no proof that I shouldn't have to do them.

8. HOW TO BEAT THE ODDS AND FIND SHAMELESS HAPPINESS EVERY DAY

The habit of forming opinions that are demanding and exaggerated seems to be universal – we all do it. There are some strong arguments that suggest the tendency has a biological basis, that we inherited the habit from our ancient ancestors. The universal nature of this tendency means that nearly everyone on the planet is missing out on happiness.

The good news is that you don't have to miss out. By being aware of the habit and knowing how to break it, you can beat the odds and find happiness every day.

Let's look at the evidence that shows how universal the habit of forming exaggerated and demanding opinions seems to be.

- Take a look around you. Probably everyone you know, as well as people you see on the street or on television, from time to time experience unhealthy negative emotions and act in ways that sabotage their goals.

- No matter where you live, you'll probably find that the cultural norms go beyond recommending certain behaviors and traditions. The people around you will insist – demand – that you obey the laws of the district and will scream blue, bloody murder if you don't.

- How many people do you know – including yourself – who have tried and failed to break a habit such as smoking or procrastination? Millions of people want to break habits and have the help of books, parents, peers, and the mass media. Still they fail.

- Many people know that their habits, such as drinking too much or over eating, are bad for them, yet they keep on doing it.

- Some people manage to break their bad habits. But months or years later they go back to them.

- It seems that it's much easier to keep bad habits, such as throwing a temper tantrum or gambling, than it is to break them.

- Even psychologists, who presumably know more about breaking bad habits than anyone else, have bad habits of their own. Many of them – along with the rest of the population – smoke, don't exercise, drink too much and are prone to depression, angry outbursts, and anxiety attacks.

All this evidence indicates that you are not alone in forming opinions that are exaggerated and demanding. Unlike most people, you now (1) are aware of the habit, (2) know how harmful the habit is, and – most importantly – (3) know how to convert your demanding and exaggerated opinions into a more reasonable outlook. This unfair advantage puts you well ahead of the game.

9. HOW TO MULTIPLY YOUR HAPPINESS

Demands and exaggerated opinions are not given up easily, and at first it may seem that your new outlook on life doesn't help; that no matter how much you argue with your demands and exaggerations, you may still feel angry, depressed, and afraid. That's because forming exaggerated and demanding opinions is a natural human habit.

Habits remain habits as long as you do nothing about them. But you can break them if you're willing to put in the effort. If you argue, over and over, with the opinions that make you feel bad, you will feel better and become more efficient and effective at solving your problems. You'll start to experience greater happiness, more often, and for longer periods of time. You will multiply your happiness.

Because you have inherited the tendency to form exaggerated and demanding opinions, you'll have to work hard to break the habit. A half-hearted, wishy-washy adherence to the new beliefs will be of little help to you. Your exaggerated and demanding opinions seem to be hardwired into you, so you must force yourself – yes, force yourself – to strongly and firmly believe that your new outlook on life makes sense and is true.

When you state your new beliefs, state them forcefully. Use

strong language – throw in the odd swear word, if it helps. Don't be afraid to say the new beliefs out loud. Repeat them to yourself over and over. Each time you say the new beliefs, change the word that you emphasize; see how the change of emphasis subtly changes the meaning. Don't merely parrot the new beliefs; think – really think hard – about what your new outlook means and how it can change your life.

You then act on your new beliefs – prove to yourself that you really believe them – over and over. As Albert Ellis was fond of saying, "Work, work, work! Practice, practice, practice!"

You won't bake a cake by merely reading the recipe: you have to follow the directions. Similarly, you won't find shameless happiness by reading this book: you have to do the work. You have to get rid of your demands and your exaggerations.

10. A LITTLE-KNOWN WAY TO CHANGE YOUR LIFE

The most common demands that we make are about ourselves, other people, and the world in general.

- I must do well and win the approval of others for my performances or else I am no good.
- Other people must treat me considerately, fairly and kindly, and in exactly the way I want them to treat me.
- I must get what I want, when I want it; and I must not get what I don't want. It's terrible if I don't get what I want, and I can't stand it.

When you dispute these particular demands and exaggerations and form more reasonable opinions about yourself, others, and life, you reach a state known as unconditional acceptance.

Acceptance is not the same as resignation. When you are resigned to something, you believe that there is nothing you can do about it. You may dwell on it and become upset over the situation. Resignation is passive but acceptance is active.

When you accept an unfortunate or inconvenient situation, (1) you recognize that the situation exists; (2) you refuse to make yourself miserable about the situation – you don't regard it as awful and you don't demand that it be different; (3) you decide whether or not you can change the situation; and (4) you either do what you can to change the situation or find ways to make yourself happy despite the situation.

When you unconditionally accept yourself, others, or life in general, you don't demand that there be an easy or perfect solution to your problems. You don't demand a quick fix. You accept that changing the situation may take some work – perhaps hard work. You accept that while the situation is unfortunate or inconvenient, it's not the end of the world.

Unconditional acceptance gives you the courage to change the things that can be changed and the serenity to live with what cannot be changed. It allows you to have peace of mind and to live in harmony with reality, even when you are fighting to change that reality.

When you accept flaws in yourself and others, you recognize that all human beings are fallible and imperfect, and that there is no reason why they should be any other way. You recognize that the flaws do not define the entire person – they are merely a part of the whole. Human beings are complex individuals; they are made up of many traits and behaviors. While you may decide that a certain trait or behavior is undesirable, you cannot decide that an entire person is undesirable. Each of us is way too complex to be given a single, global rating.

So too with life. Many things will happen to you. Some will be good; some will be bad; and some will be neither good nor bad – they will be neutral. But you cannot rate your entire life's experience as good or bad based on a single event, or even series of events. Life, like human beings, is too complex to be given a single, global rating.

When you have unconditional acceptance of yourself, others, and life, you come to conclusions that are similar to the following:

E. I wish I were more successful but my lack of success doesn't make me worthless.

E. I don't like the way you treat me but your actions do not make you evil.

E. I don't like the situation but I can find ways to be happy nevertheless.

11. ARE YOU READY FOR SHAMELESS HAPPINESS?

If you're going to be shamelessly happy, you're going to have to do more than just read this book. The pursuit of shameless happiness requires a certain degree of willpower. This raises an interesting question: What is willpower and how do you get it?

In *How to Make Yourself Happy and Remarkably Less Disturbable* (pages 39-42), Albert Ellis compares will with willpower.

Ellis makes the case that having the will to do something is little more than having a desire to do it. For example, the desire to stick to a diet, to ask someone out for a date, or to find a new job. Having the will to do it isn't enough; you need to give your will some power; i.e., you back it up with action. Ellis suggests five steps to powering your will, steps you can take to be happy:

1. You decide to be happy. This step is merely a recognition of your desire, of your will. On its own, it is insufficient. It will be the next four steps that convert your will into successful goal-attainment.
2. You make yourself determined to be happy. At this point you resolve to do whatever it takes – no matter what – to

achieve your goal.

3. You acquire knowledge about how to reach your goal. You look for times when you are sabotaging your happiness. You learn about the two early warning signs of long-term unhappiness and how to avoid them. You decide what activities you enjoy and you plan to set aside time to do the things you enjoy.

4. You put your determination and knowledge to work, and you take action. You look for your exaggerated and demanding opinions, and you dispute them until you can form and believe more reasonable opinions.

5. Most people, being fallible humans, run into trouble somewhere between Step 1 & Step 4, and fail to reach their goals. When that happens, many people quit; they give up on their goals. But willpower means that you don't quit, you merely go back to Step 1 and start again.

In the same passage that Ellis discusses willpower, he offers a word of caution that can be paraphrased as: It isn't compulsory to reach your goals – there is no reason why you absolutely must succeed. Nor does failing to reach your goals make you a failure. People who reach their goals have no more worth than other people who fail to reach theirs. Goals give you a sense of direction, they are your guide to a joyous and fulfilling life. Don't make them into your master.

Here's what Albert Ellis has to say about willpower:

"Willpower, again, means the action, the work that you do to add power to your will. There may be another way to get it – without work. But I doubt it. Life rarely offers shortcuts!"

I like to think of willpower as a verb. It is something you do – not something you have. You give power to your will; you give power to your desire to be happy. You set your goals and you work and persist until you make them happen.

12. THE THREE TIMELESS PRINCIPLES OF SHAMELESS HAPPINESS

Let me repeat something I said near the start of this book. Shameless happiness is a commitment you make to yourself to refuse to be miserable, while unapologetically and unreservedly making yourself happy at every opportunity. Shameless happiness is the pursuit of an ethical, rewarding, and joyous life that is guided by compassion and reason.

When you put into practice the ideas discussed in this book, you will gain three immediate benefits:

- Your feelings of happiness will be stronger;
- You will feel happy more often; and
- Your happiness will last longer.

To make yourself shamelessly happy, remind yourself and put into practice the three timeless principles of shameless happiness:

1. You feel the way you think. Your feelings do not come from other people, outside forces, or events; you create them with your thoughts and your beliefs. By committing yourself to thinking in ways that are non-demanding and not exaggerated you can refuse to be miserable and make yourself happy at every opportunity.

2. You sabotage your own happiness with demands and exaggerations. You can dramatically and permanently increase your happiness by getting rid of your demands and exaggerations. You get rid of your demands and exaggerations by vigorously disputing them and consistently acting in ways that contradict them.

3. A lifetime of shameless happiness requires a commitment. A wishy-washy, half-hearted attempt to be happy will probably fail. If you want shameless happiness, make it a habit to use the principles and methods outlined in this book each and every day. No one can do it for you. It's up to you!

13. HOW TO BE HAPPY FOR THE REST OF YOUR LIFE

Many people think they must know what the future holds in store for them. They are convinced that they cannot stand uncertainty. Their opinion of the future is distorted by the demand for certainty and an exaggerated, negative opinion of uncertainty.

Life comes with only one guarantee: one day you will die. Everything else in life – including life itself – is on loan to us. The good times and the bad, they come and they go. Moments of happiness and moments of pain; famines and feasts; beauty and ugliness; good health and illness; love and enmity. All of these are temporary. No one can predict when they will come; no one can predict when they will end. The passages of life are ruled by one maxim: This, too, shall pass.

Demanding to know what tomorrow will bring is a recipe for misery. So, too, is demanding that tomorrow must bring you what you desire. By all means, hang on to your wishes, your hopes, and your dreams, and do all you can to make them come true. But do so while accepting that nothing is certain, nothing is guaranteed, and nothing is promised.

Living with uncertainty does not have to be bleak. Despite

the constraints of uncertainty, you have within you the power to lead a rewarding, ethical, and joyous life. How?

- Take the time to create a list of the activities you enjoy and find rewarding. What are your hobbies, your interests, your passions? What causes do you feel strongly about? What would you like to know more about? Where would you like to travel? With whom do you want to spend your time? If you had more money, what would you buy, and to what – if anything – would you contribute your finances?

- Decide – or, better yet, determine – to spend as much of your time and energies as you can in pursuit of these activities. Think short-term and long-term. What do you want to do in the next thirty minutes, and what do you want to be able to do when you're sixty-four?

- Accept that there are some things you will probably never do, but for everything else: Just do it!

It would take several lifetimes to try all the activities that are available to us. For example, if you spent your entire life studying mathematics, you would still not know all there is to know about the subject. There is just too much to do for any one individual to have tried everything humanly possible.

Life is temporary. From the beginning of time (if there is such a thing) until a few decades ago, you did not exist. In a few more decades, you will once again cease to exist. From the beginning of time, until the end of time, non-existence is your natural state. Life is a brief interruption to your natural state of non-existence. This brief interruption provides you with an opportunity to learn, an opportunity to explore, and, especially, an opportunity to experience.

Life is an opportunity that most don't get. At the time you were conceived, millions of your father's sperm raced to meet your mother's ovum. Had another sperm won the race, you would not be here. Two to three hundred million of your potential brothers and sisters did not get the opportunity you got (and that's not counting all the other times your mother released an unfertilized egg, or all the other times your father ejaculated). There is no law that says you must make the most of this opportunity. You can, if you wish, spend your life isolated in your living room, getting drunk, while watching soap operas. However, given the rarity of your opportunity, it is probably best to live life as fully as you can.

I have found it useful to think of life as being like a vacation in a foreign land. It's an opportunity to learn the language, to examine the culture, to learn to dance, to experience the music, to sample the food, to fall in love, to learn about the universe and the various life forms, to read, to go sightseeing, to marvel at the latest technologies, to meet and learn about other people, to learn new skills, to understand and appreciate mathematics and the sciences, etc.

While we're here, we not only have the opportunity to enjoy ourselves, we may also take the responsibility to share what we have learned, and to do what we can for the welfare of our fellow voyagers.

And then, as with any vacation, there comes a time to go home; or in the case of life, there comes a time to return to our natural state of non-existence.

During your time here, you don't have to prove yourself. You don't have to impress anybody, including yourself. You may make as many mistakes as you want. Similarly, other people do not have to live by your rules and expectations. And life does not have to be fair or easy.

Imagine going on a vacation and being miserable the entire time. It would hardly be worth it, would it? Far better to cram every possible moment with rewarding, joyful experiences. So it is with life: It makes sense to stubbornly refuse to make yourself miserable and to enjoy this life – the only one you can be sure of – as much as you can.

Decide to make the most of every day because although you may not be enjoying yourself at this moment, you have no way of knowing what tomorrow holds. Once you're dead, you're dead and have no hope of ever being able to enjoy yourself. While you remain alive there is always the possibility of happiness. Death takes away that possibility forever.

Disputing your demands and exaggerations, along with

purposeful physical activity, is the best path to shameless happiness (although as Stephen Hawking has demonstrated, even movement is unnecessary for a rewarding and joyous life that is well worth living). The more you do with your time, the more you are likely to enjoy shameless happiness.

Life offers so many opportunities and so little time to follow them. In his book, *Affirmations: Joyful and Creative Exuberance*, Paul Kurtz wrote:

"The meaning of life is not to be found in a secret formula discovered by ancient prophets or modern gurus who withdraw from living to seek quiet contemplation and release. Life has no meaning per se; it does, however, present us with innumerable opportunities, which we can either squander and retreat from in fear or seize with exuberance."

Given that this is the only life we will ever have, it makes sense to milk it for all we can get. There is no second time around. *Carpe diem*!

ABOUT THE AUTHOR

Will Ross taught himself how to use Rational Emotive Behavior Therapy (REBT) and now teaches other REBT self-helpers. He is the author and publisher of online REBT self-help materials and the co-founder of the REBT Network, a major online resource for REBT practitioners, their clients, and students of REBT. This is how he describes his work:

"When Albert Ellis created Rational Emotive Behavior Therapy in the 1950's, he created one of the first self-help therapies. Many people can teach themselves REBT as I did, but some people need extra help. That's what I do: I tutor people who want extra help. Over the years, I've created a number of self-help tools and written a number of articles designed to help people help themselves with REBT. I also work privately, one-on-one, with those who request it, helping them to remain focused and master the techniques and philosophy so that they can overcome their problems, reach their goals, and lead a rewarding and joyous life."

Made in the USA
Las Vegas, NV
07 June 2021

24355618R00024